What is it like now?

On journeys

Heinemann LIBRARY

Tony Pickford

www.heinemann.co.uk/library
Visit our website to find out more information about Heinemann Library books.

To order:
Phone 44 (0) 1865 888066
Send a fax to 44 (0) 1865 314091
Visit the Heinemann Bookshop at www.heinemann.co.uk/library to browse our catalogue and order online.

First published in Great Britain by Heinemann Library, Halley Court, Jordan Hill, Oxford OX2 8EJ, a division of Reed Educational and Professional Publishing Ltd. Heinemann is a registered trademark of Reed Educational & Professional Publishing Ltd.

OXFORD MELBOURNE AUCKLAND JOHANNESBURG BLANTYRE
GABORONE IBADAN PORTSMOUTH (NH) USA CHICAGO

Designed by Celia Floyd
Illustrations by Jo Brooker
Originated by Dot Gradations
Printed in Hong Kong/China

ISBN 0 431 15001 X (hardback)
07 06 05 04 03
10 9 8 7 6 5 4 3 2 1

ISBN 0 431 15007 9 (paperback)
07 06 05 04 03
10 9 8 7 6 5 4 3 2 1

British Library Cataloguing in Publication Data
Pickford, Tony
What is it like on journeys
1. Voyages and travels – Juvenile literature
I. Title
910

Acknowledgements
The Publishers would like to thank the following for permission to reproduce photographs: Bubbles: Jennie Woodcock p9; Collections: Michael StMaur Sheil p7, Lawrence Engelsberg p12, Liz Stares pp17, 19; Eye Ubiquitous: Bob Battersby p8, Paul Seheult p15; John Birdsall Photography: pp4, 18; Sally and Richard Greenhill pp5, 11, 16, 25; Skyscan Photolibrary: Quick UK Ltd pp22, 23; Sylvia Cordaiy Photo Library: John Farmar p24, Jonathan Smith p26, P Cridland p27; Tografox: P & O Stena 20, 21, R D Battersby pp10, 13, 14

Cover photograph reproduced with permission of Barry Lewis/Network.

Every effort has been made to contact copyright holders of any material reproduced in this book. Any omissions will be rectified in subsequent printings if notice is given to the Publisher.

Contents

Words printed in **bold letters like these** are explained in the Glossary.

Why do people go on journeys?

Do you enjoy going on a journey? People go on journeys for many reasons.

- They might want to buy something from a shop or meet some friends.
- They might travel by train or bus to get to where they work. Some people have jobs which mean that they have to travel around.

These children are walking to school together. This is a safe and healthy way to get to school.

- Some children have to travel quite a long way to get to school. Others live near to their school so only need to make a short journey.
- Some families go on long journeys when they go away on holiday. They travel by road to the seaside or by air to another country.

This family is going away on holiday. They are climbing the steps into an aeroplane.

This book looks at some of the different ways of travelling and some of the things that you will see and do when you go on a journey.

Different ways of travelling

The way we travel often depends on how far we have to go. On a short journey you might walk, or go by bus or bicycle. For longer journeys, your family may go by bus, car or train.

For a long journey, especially to another country, you might travel on an aeroplane. You may go on a special kind of ship called a **ferry**. Ferries can carry **vehicles** as well as people.

Riding a bike is good fun, but you should always wear a helmet when you go onto the roads near your home.

You can also travel to **Europe** by train using a **tunnel**. The tunnel has been built under the sea from Britain to France. It is called the Channel Tunnel.

The vehicle that you use will also depend on where you live. What forms of transport have you used?

This ship is called a ferry. It carries people and vehicles from Britain to France.

Going to school

Many children walk to school because it is quite near to their home. They go with their parents so that they are safe. There is often a school crossing patrol to help children across busy roads.

For some children school is too far away to walk. They might have to travel by bicycle, car, bus or train.

The school crossing patrol stops the traffic so that these children can cross the road safely.

Some children travel by bus to get to school.

In the countryside, a school might have children coming to it from a very wide area. A bus will pick children up from small villages and farms and take them to and from school every day.

If there is no bus to take children to school, then children in the country might have to travel in a **four-wheel drive vehicle** or even on a tractor. How do you get to school?

Journeys to school

Children who live in different places will see different things on their journeys to school. Some children live in towns and walk to school. One of their parents walks with them every day.

They walk along the **pavement** beside a busy road and pass shops, a church and the local park.

This girl lives in a town and walks to school every day.

These children have just arrived at their school. They have travelled there by car.

Other children live in the country. Their mum or dad takes them to school in a car. The school is not a long way away, but the narrow country roads are too dangerous for them to walk along. There are no pavements to walk on.

Children who live in the country might pass a field of cows every day. They might also pass a church.

Local journeys

Your mum or dad might have to travel quite a long way to get to where they work. Sometimes they might have to use different forms of transport for different parts of the journey.

Your mum or dad might travel to a railway station by car and catch a train into the city centre. Then they might have to travel on an underground train or a **tram** to get to where they work.

This tram in Manchester travels on metal tracks through the streets of the city.

Big supermarkets can often be found on the edge of towns. People have to travel to them in their cars.

People also make journeys to do their shopping or to visit a swimming pool or leisure centre. There are often big supermarkets in and around towns. There are car parks for people to leave their cars while they do their shopping.

Planning a long journey by car

If you are going on a long journey it is best to plan the journey first. If you are going by car you can use maps to help you decide which way to go. A road atlas contains maps that show towns and villages and the roads in between. It is often quickest to find roads which go around busy towns and cities.

A road atlas helps you to plan journeys so that you go by the quickest route.

You can use a computer program to help you to plan a journey. The computer program shows you the best road to take.

Before you set out, you can check if there are any road-works by looking at **Teletext** on your television. If you listen to the radio when you are travelling, it will tell you where the **traffic jams** are.

This family are loading up their car before they go on a long journey.

On the journey

A long journey by car can be exciting at first. Later on it can get very tiring. It helps if you have games to play and things to do.

One game to play is I-Spy where you look for things beginning with a different letter. If you pick 'T', for example, then you might see a tree or traffic lights. Can you think of anything else beginning with 'T', that you might see?

Car journeys can be boring unless you have games to play.

This road sign shows that the road ahead is going to be very bendy.

You could look for different road signs. Some road signs are like simple maps. They show the shape of the road ahead. These signs are in the shape of a triangle.

It is important on a long journey to take a break so that the driver does not get too tired. You can stop at a service area where there are places to eat, toilets, a shop and a petrol filling station.

A journey by train

If you are planning a journey by train you will need a timetable, which tells you when trains leave the station to go to different places.

A train journey can be more exciting than a journey by car. You sit in a **railway carriage** that is pulled by the train's engine. There is more room to move around in a carriage than in a car. You can walk along the train to buy a drink or a snack.

These children are enjoying a journey by train because they can talk and play more easily than in a car.

A train can travel very fast. Towns, villages and the countryside seem to pass by very quickly.

You get a very different view from a railway carriage than from a car window. You can look down on fields, roads and houses. Have you ever made a journey by train?

*On a journey by train, you might see a busy **junction** with lots of trains coming together.*

A journey by sea

Sometimes people need to travel by sea to go from one part of the country to another. This is done by taking a special ship called a **ferry**.

One journey you might make is by ferry from Stranraer in Scotland to Belfast in Northern Ireland. When the ferry gets into the **harbour**, cars, lorries and buses can drive on board.

Jets of water shoot out of the back of the Fastferry to send it across the water.

On board the ship there is a play area, a shop and different places to eat.

The ferry leaves the harbour and travels slowly out into the Irish Sea. Once it is out to sea, it speeds up and shoots jets of water out of the back so that it skims across the sea.

From the back of the ferry, you can see land slowly disappearing from view. But very soon, more land appears and the ferry slows down again to go up Belfast **Lough** into Belfast.

A journey by air

A journey by air is a quick way of travelling very long distances. Have you ever travelled in an aeroplane or been to an airport? An airport is a place where aeroplanes land and take off. It has runways and a building where people collect their tickets and hand over their bags.

These aeroplanes are loading and unloading their passengers at an airport.

An airport takes up a lot of space. When a new runway is built, a lot of land is taken over and trees have to be cut down. Sometimes people who live near an airport complain about the noise that aeroplanes make.

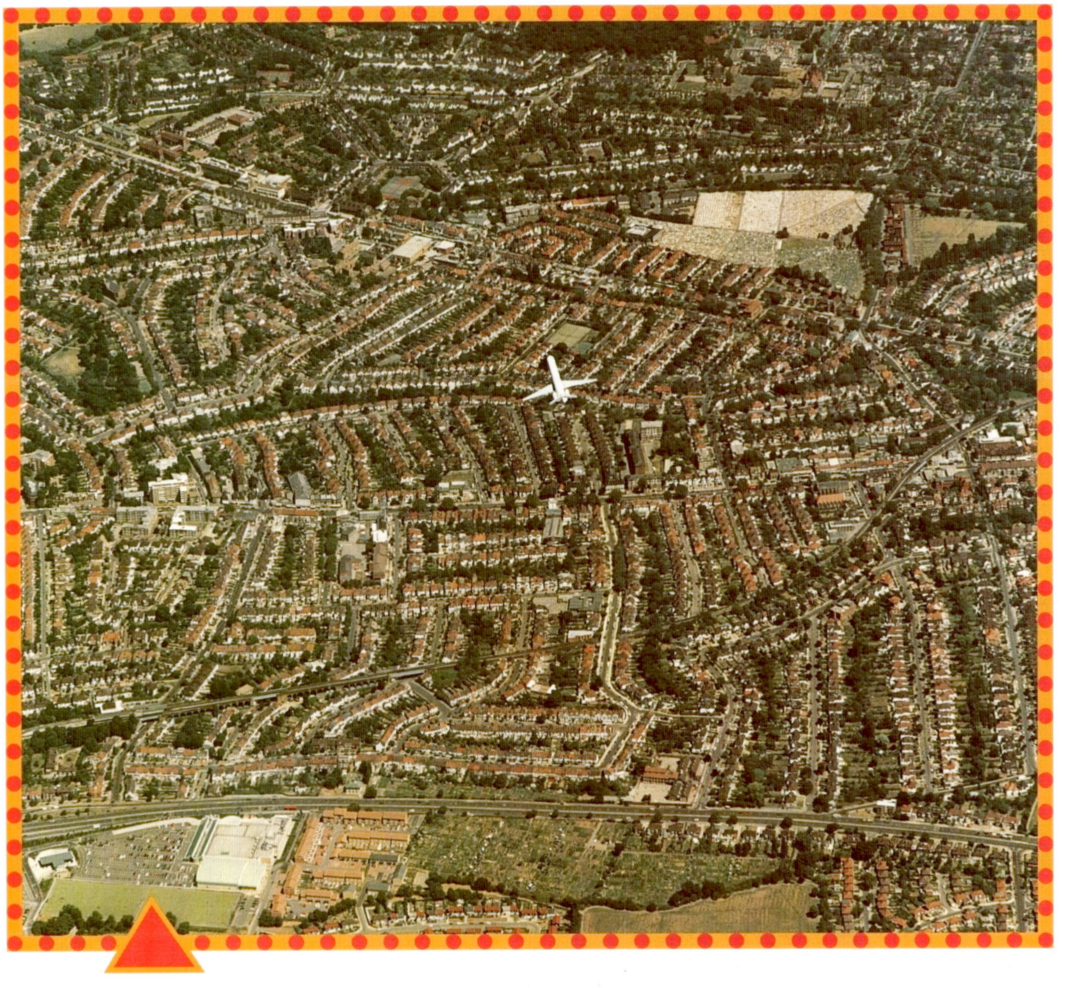

When you look out of the windows of an aeroplane the land below looks like a map with streets and houses laid out.

Cars and pollution

When lots of people take their cars on journeys at the same time, the roads become very busy. Sometimes there are so many **vehicles** on a road at the same time that they have to slow down and stop. This is called a **traffic jam**. People can become angry if they are stuck in a traffic jam for a long time.

There are so many cars and lorries on this road that they have had to stop and wait.

Journeys by car cause **pollution**. Cars can be noisy and they also give out **fumes** that can make the air dirty. The fumes can make some people cough and become ill.

It is a good idea to make journeys by bicycle, bus and train whenever we can. If there are fewer cars on the road, there will be fewer traffic jams, less noise and less pollution.

If people travel by bus or cycle, then there are fewer cars on the road and less pollution.

The end of a journey

When you travel by car, train, **ferry** or aeroplane to another place, you may find that it seems very different from the place where you live.

If you look around you will see that most places are the same in some important ways. Most houses will have walls, a roof and rooms for a family to live in just like your home.

The weather might be warmer and buildings might be built from different materials when you are in a different country.

The land might look different, but you will find that people use the land to grow **crops** or keep animals just like in Britain. School buildings might be smaller or larger than your school, but there are schools everywhere.

When you go to another country, see if you can find any other ways in which it is like the place where you live.

Farmers in distant places may keep different animals to those that we keep in Britain.

Activities

Does your family have a car? List the journeys your family makes every week. Are there any car journeys that could be done in another way?

What is your favourite journey? Perhaps it is the trip to the shops or the swimming pool or when you go on holiday. Draw or paint a picture that shows your favourite journey. Try to put in all the interesting things that you see.

Your favourite journey might be a trip to the swimming pool.

What is your journey to school like? What things do you see on the way to school every day? Draw a map to show your journey to school. Try to make it simple and clear so that someone else could find their way.

Your journey to school might look something like this.

Find out for yourself

Places to visit

There are lots of museums that you can visit to find out about transport in the past and the different forms of transport that we have today.

- National Railway Museum
  Leeman Rd
  York YO26 4XY
- National Waterways Museum
  Llanthony Warehouse
  Gloucester Docks
  Gloucester GL1 2EH

Books

Linkers: Journeys discovered through Geography, Karen Bryant-Mole, A & C Black, 2001

What was it like in the past? On journeys, Mandy Ross, Heinemann Library, 2002

Glossary

crops plants that a farmer grows to sell as food

Europe a group of countries that includes France and Germany

ferry a boat or ship which takes people from one side of a piece of water to another

four-wheel drive vehicle a car or van with an engine that drives all four wheels

fumes strong-smelling gas or smoke

harbour a sheltered area of water where ships come in

junction a place where roads or railways meet

Lough a lake or part of the sea that has land on three sides

materials what something is made of, for example, wood

pavement the part at each side of a street for people to walk along safely

pollution dirty and unhealthy air and water

railway carriage a vehicle that carries people on rails

Teletext pages of text on a television screen

traffic jam when there are lots of vehicles on the road at the same time

tram a vehicle on rails that carries people around the streets of a town or city

tunnel a long hole under the ground

vehicle any thing which takes people and things from one place to another on land. Cars, buses and lorries are all vehicles.

Index